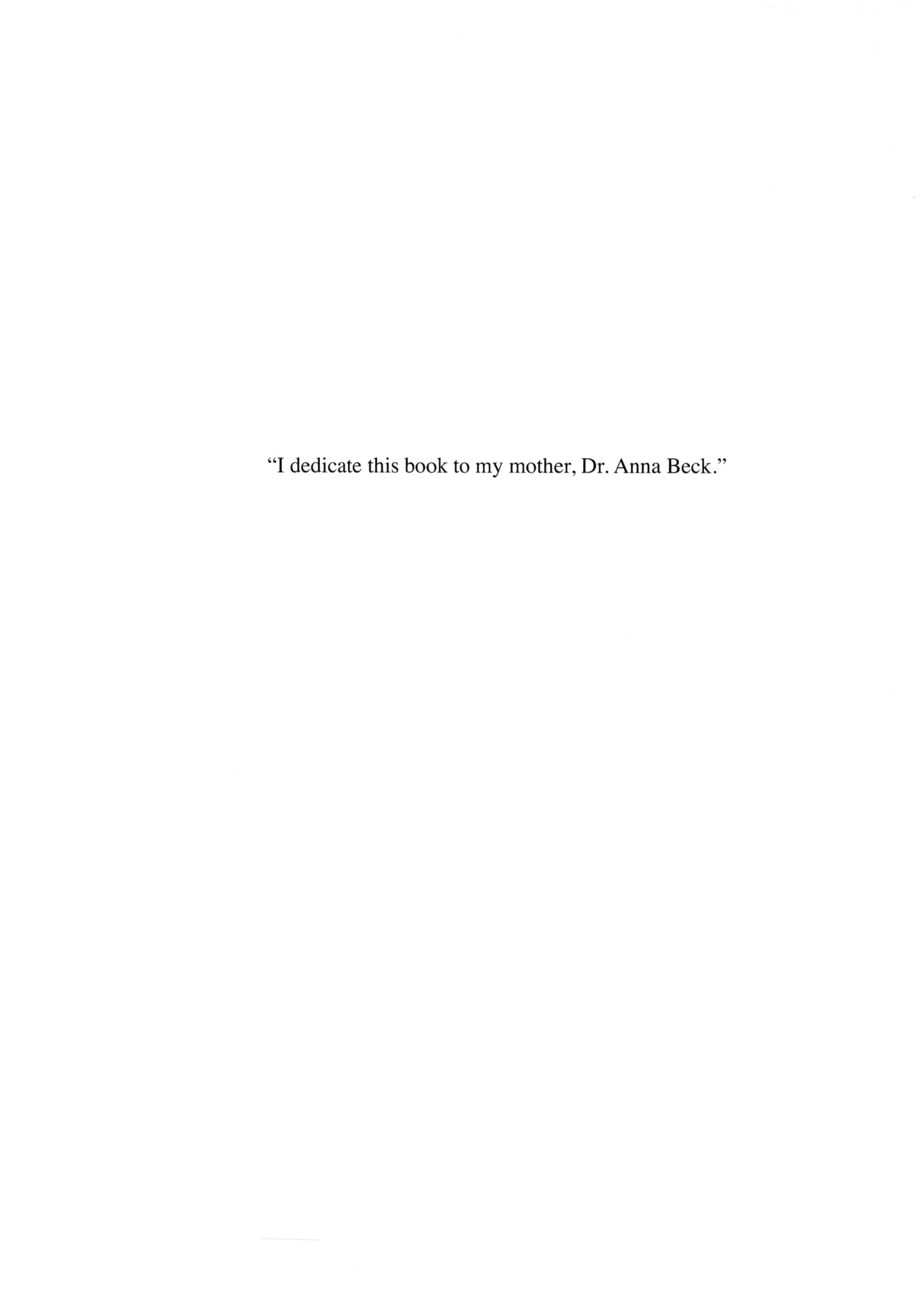

“I dedicate this book to my mother, Dr. Anna Beck.”

Grace And The Flag

By Lauren Lundin

Cricket Cottage Publishing, LLC

Forinformationaboutgroupsalesandpermission,contact Cricket Cottage Publishing, LLC

Website address: www.thecricketpublishing.com

ISBN 978-0-9991224-4-0

In a small town near Baltimore, Maryland, spotted with green forests and rolling hills, lived a girl who was curious about the world around her.

She wanted to climb trees, go fishing and spend her evenings trapping toads and fireflies with her bare hands.

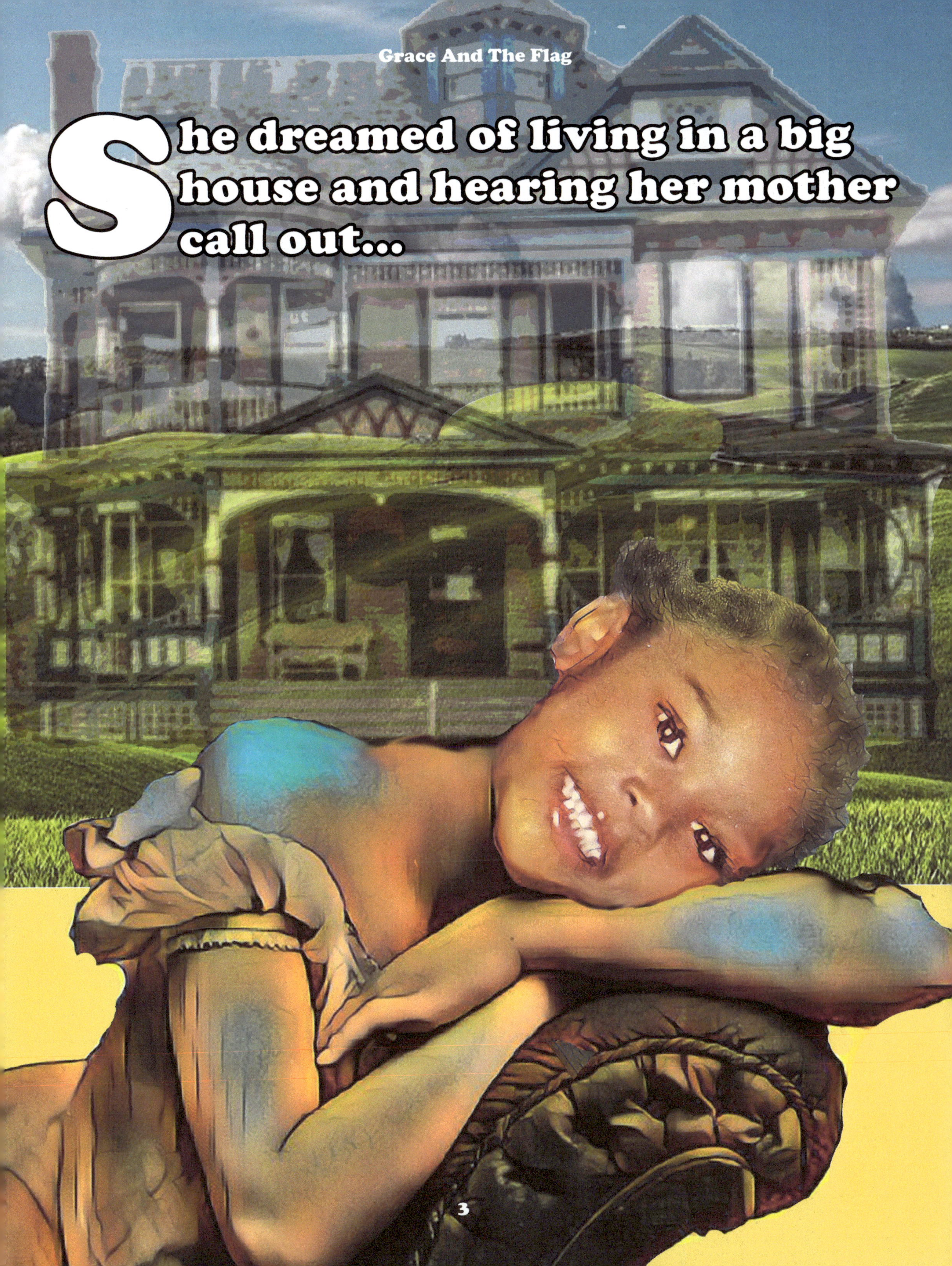

She dreamed of living in a big house and hearing her mother call out...

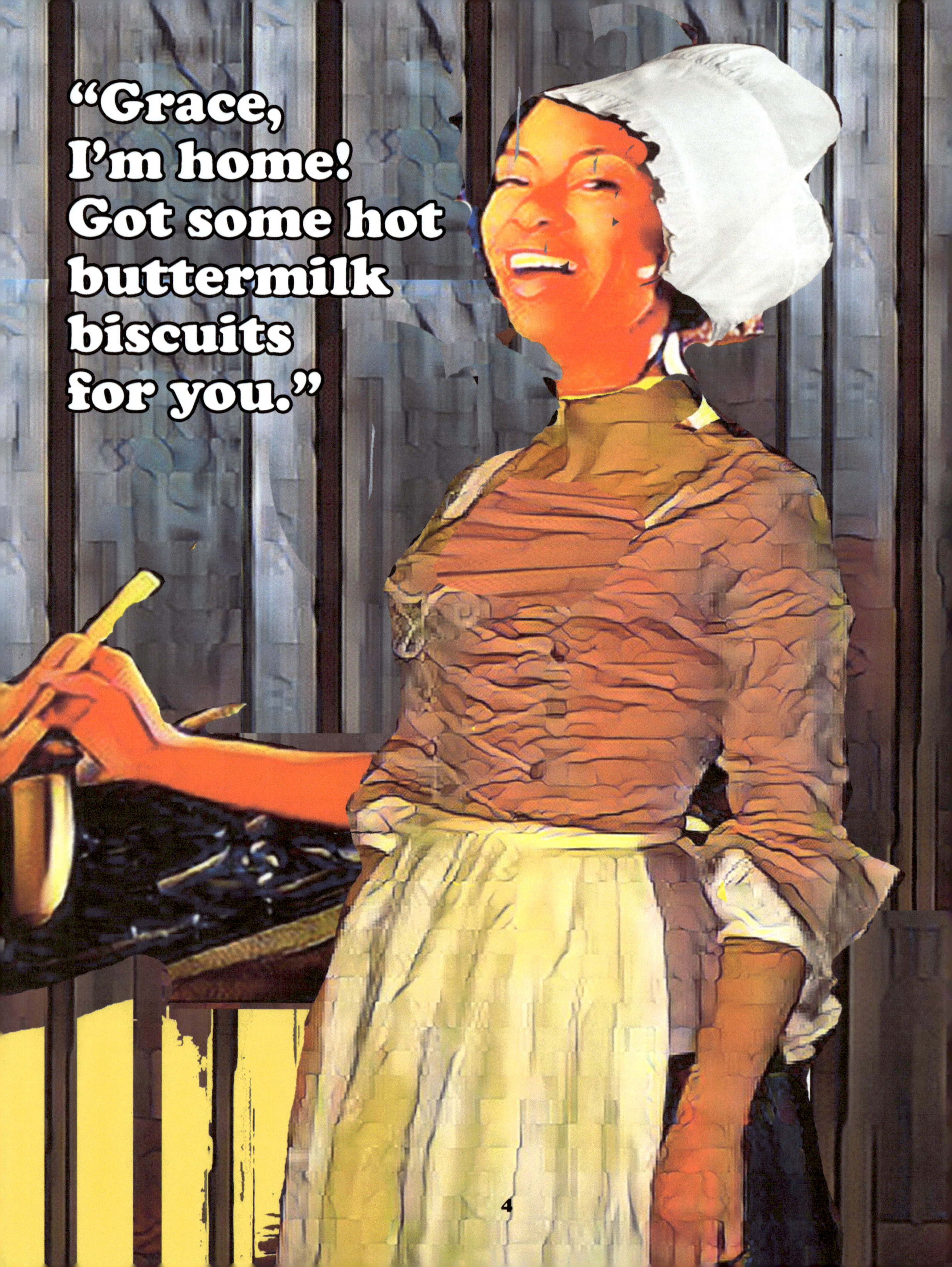
"Grace,
I'm home!
Got some hot
buttermilk
biscuits
for you."

Grace wanted to spend her days chasing rabbits all the way to the other side of the smokestacks and wandering along different paths to find the best tree to climb.

She wanted to happen upon Miss Bertha and Mr. Jim on the way to church and spin in her new frilly dress while they smiled and said, "You look lovely today Grace."

However, life for Grace and her mother was not easy and carefree. Money was scarce, food was sparse and their home was made of wooden boards and branches. They lived the challenging life of free slaves.

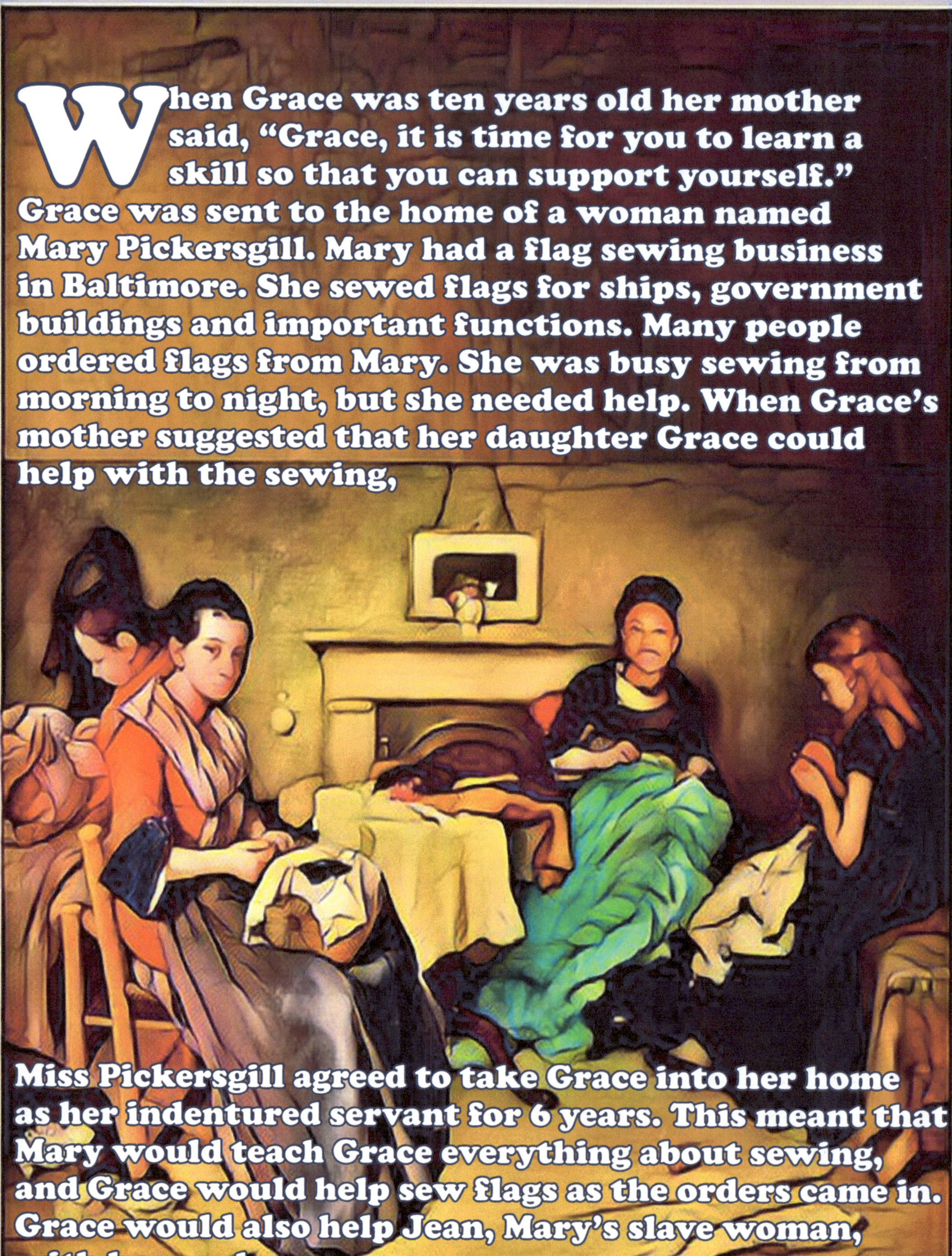

When Grace was ten years old her mother said, "Grace, it is time for you to learn a skill so that you can support yourself." Grace was sent to the home of a woman named Mary Pickersgill. Mary had a flag sewing business in Baltimore. She sewed flags for ships, government buildings and important functions. Many people ordered flags from Mary. She was busy sewing from morning to night, but she needed help. When Grace's mother suggested that her daughter Grace could help with the sewing,

Miss Pickersgill agreed to take Grace into her home as her indentured servant for 6 years. This meant that Mary would teach Grace everything about sewing, and Grace would help sew flags as the orders came in. Grace would also help Jean, Mary's slave woman, with house chores.

One day Army commander, Major General George Armistead, came to Mary's house bearing fruit as a gift and a very special request. The fruit was called a grapefruit. Grace had never seen or tasted a grapefruit before. It was a strange fruit, almost as big as her head! And the request? General Armistead wanted Mary to create a flag.

Not just any flag, but an American flag. A flag that stood as tall as a house - measuring 30 feet by 42 feet. A flag so large that it could easily been seen from a distance. What a project!

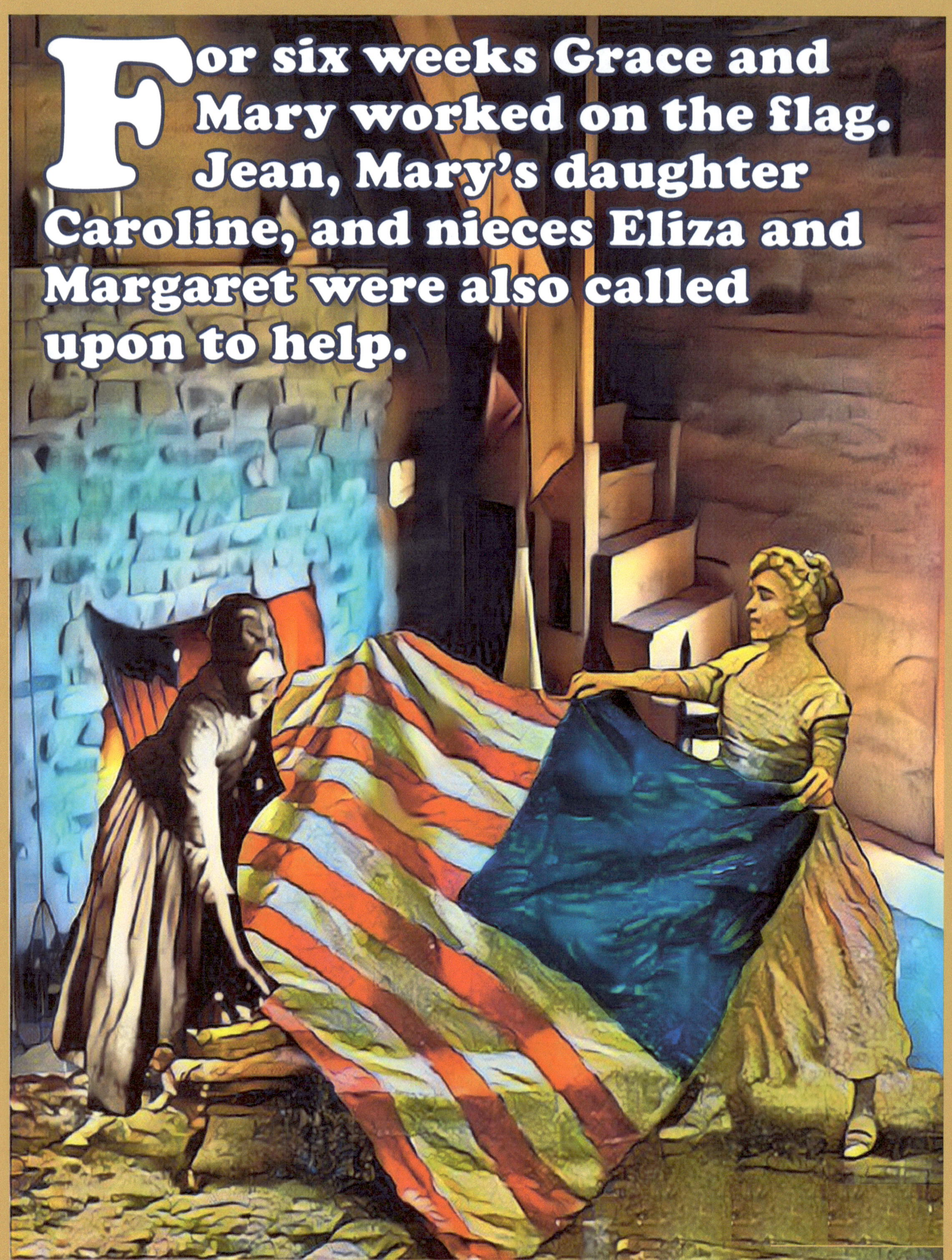

For six weeks Grace and Mary worked on the flag. Jean, Mary's daughter Caroline, and nieces Eliza and Margaret were also called upon to help.

Grace's favorite part of the project was sewing on the 15 stars, one for each state. She secured the stars with pins to ensure they could be sewn perfectly into place. As she worked, she learned the name of each state and wondered what life was like in each one.

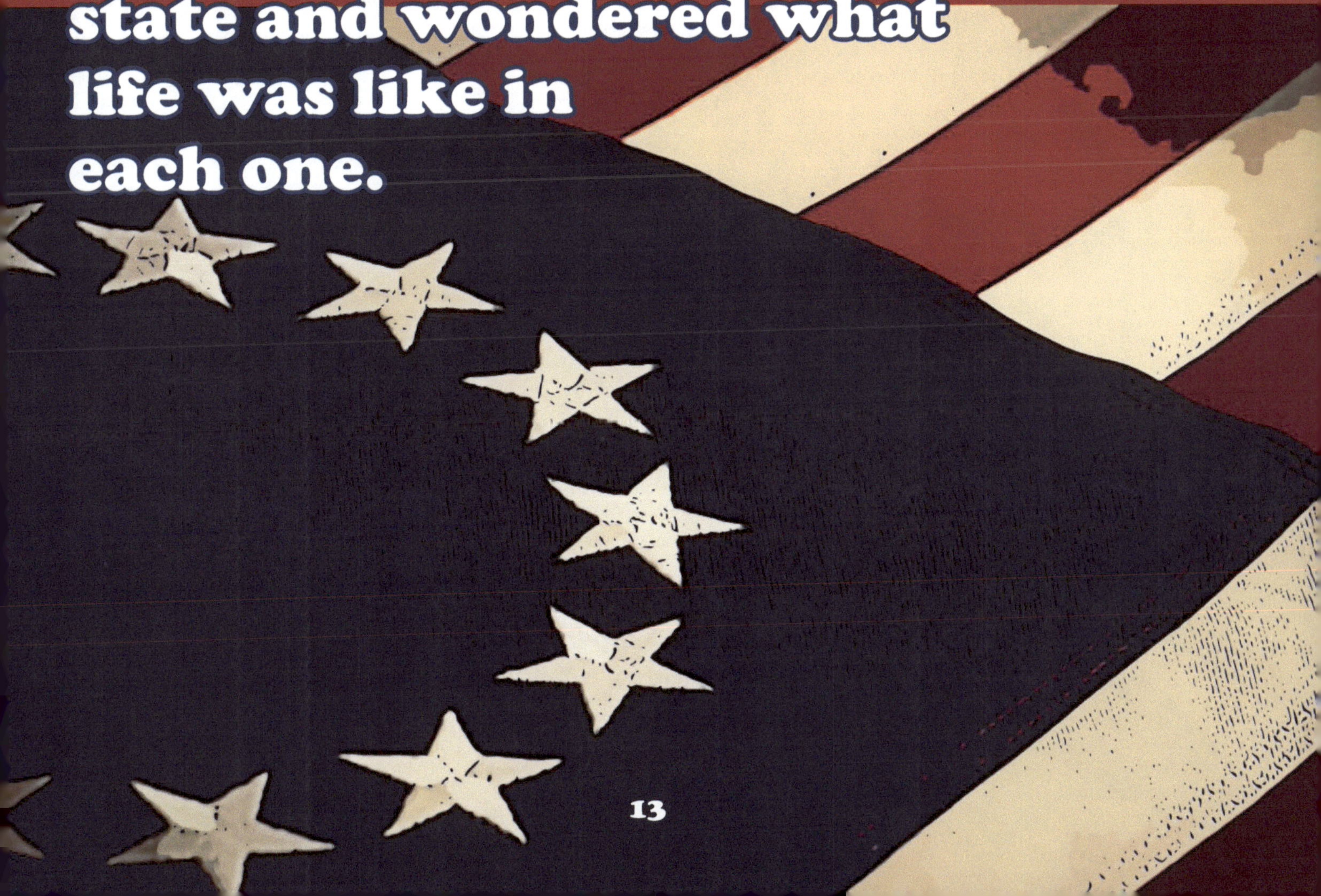

When the flag was finished in 1813 and hung high over Fort McHenry in Baltimore Harbor, Grace was proud of her contribution to this historic symbol. Everyone who saw the flag was amazed by its majestic beauty.

In September 1814, as this majestic flag flew high over Fort McHenry and endured a British bombardment during the Battle of Baltimore, Francis Scott Key was so inspired that he wrote a poem that later became the "The Star Spangled Banner" which is now America's national anthem.

The American flag represents different things to different people. For Grace, it represented hard work and accomplishment. For others today, it represents struggle, sacrifice and determination. And still for others, it represents freedom, equality and the chance for positive change. America has a colorful history and the flag connects us together in special ways. We can all be proud of the contributions made by remarkable people like Grace Wisher.

The End

Ten Questions About the American Flag

See if You Can You Answer Them.

1. What does your flag mean to you?

2. How do you feel connected to your flag?

3. What do the stars on the flag represent?

4. What do the stripes represent?

5. What do the colors on the flag represent; red, white, blue?

6. Why did this flag have 15 stars and 15 stripes?

7. How is the current United States Flag different from the flag that Grace Wisher helped create?

8. Where/What types of places can you always find the United States Flag flying?

9. Where can this flag be found today?

10. Who asked Mary Pickersgill to sew the garrison flag that flew over Fort McHenry in 1814?

Words Used in this Book

1. FORT MCHENRY:

A military fort in Maryland at the entrance to Baltimore's harbor, best known as a stronghold against British troops during the Battle of Baltimore.

2. GARRISON FLAG:
The largest
size of the American flag
flown on holidays and
special occasions.

3. INDENTURED SERVANT:
A person who signs a contract
for an established period of
time and must work
for the holder of the contract
typically in return
for food and a place to live.

4. SLAVE:
A person who is the property
of someone and is forced
to obey/work for them.

5. THE STAR-SPANGLED BANNER:
The national anthem of
the United States of America,
written by Francis Scott Key
in 1814.

About the Author

Lauren Lundin is an international guidance counselor, wife, and mother of three little girls. She was born in Thailand, raised in India, and has lived in many different countries. Her graduate studies at Columbia University in New York focused on cross cultural awareness, microaggressions, and multicultural understanding.

As a mixed-race woman (African American and Caucasian), she is particularly interested in race-related history and the evolution of minority groups. She values the opportunity to encourage and support the learning of all children. Lauren is also the author of another top-rated children's book called My Toothbrush Ran Away (ISBN 978-94-022-4098-6), which teaches kids about the importance of good dental hygiene.

A Note from the Publisher

Thank you for purchasing, reading, and enjoying Grace and The Flag by Lauren Lundin. We know you could have gone elsewhere to select your reading material, so we are honored that you gave us the opportunity to entertain, educate, inform, and impact you. If you enjoyed this story, please go to Amazon.com and write a favorable review of this book and Lauren Lundin and encourage your family and friends to buy their own copies. These are two of the best things you can do to help Lauren gain notoriety, sell more books, and write more stories. If you'd like to get a special message or comment directly to Lauren about this book or anything else, you can do so by going to our website and leaving us your name and contact information. We'll alert you about new books from Lauren and other Cricket Cottage authors, characters, and books. We may even give you sneak peeks and special discounts that aren't generally available to the public.

Again, thanks for reading Cricket Cottage Publishing, LLC. We look forward to bringing you more stories that entertain, educate, inform and impact!

Cricket Cottage Publishing, LLC

www.ingramcontent.com/pod-product-compliance
Lightning Source LLC
LaVergne TN
LVHW070225110826
845147LV00003B/648

9780999122440